How To
Forget Unwanted
Memories

Michael A. Danforth

How To Forget Unwanted Memories

How To Forget Unwanted Memories

Thank you to my lovely and artistic granddaughter Gabrielle Martinez for her amazing book cover and design.

Thank you Karriana Allum for your help in editing this book.

Thank You to Craig Danforth (founder of Frugalgoogle.com) for helping with graphics and other miscellaneous work needed to get this book in print.

A special thank you to my wife, Tamera Danforth and sister-in-love, Sheryl Jones. Together, they continuously work hard to keep my life in order. I truly appreciate their help to finalize this book for print.

For information regarding permissions to reproduce material from this book, please email or write:

Michael A. Danforth

Mountain Top International

PO Box 43

Yakima, Washington 98907

www.mticenter.com

Table of Contents

CHAPTER 1

A Prophet's Quest for Restoration

You might wonder, why a person who functions primarily in the office of a prophet is writing a book on how to forget unwanted memories. The answer is quite simple: I'm on a quest toward full restoration.

For years, I have witnessed a level of dysfunction in various ministries in the body of Christ, including my own. Like so many, I know what it is like to deal with tormenting memories. These tormenting thoughts from the past are not just limited to the seven spheres or mountains of human society (arts and entertainment, business, education, family, government/politics, media and religion) but reach into every other field of life, whatever that may be.

Whether it's a person in business, sports, education, science or medicine, all of the above and more have struggled with a measure of unwanted memories.

For a great number of years, due to poor choices in my life, I secretly struggled with a level of mental torment, which would often lead me into tears of depression. There were times when I was doubtful that I would ever rise to a level of normality that would enable me to fulfill my purpose in life. Believe it or not, there are billions of others struggling in these same areas of their lives. Because of poor choices and abusive behavior, the world's population has developed a very high rate of mental illness.

Mental illness refers to a wide range of mental health conditions; disorders that affect your mood, thinking and behavior. Examples of mental illness include: depression, anxiety disorders, schizophrenia, eating disorders and addictive behaviors, just to name a few. Depression is the most common type of mental illness, affecting more than 26% of the U.S. adult population. It has been estimated that by the year 2020, depression will be the second leading cause of disability throughout the world, trailing only ischemic heart disease. (*worldmentalhealth.com*) These numbers do not include the increasing amount of youth who struggle with mental illness at an alarming rate.

Major depression amongst our youth in the U.S especially girls has jumped 37% in the last decade. Over 3 million adolescents in the United States, between the ages of 12-17 reported at least one major depressive episode in the last year.

This does not include the potential millions of others who have not, nor does it depict the teenage suicidal rate that reached an all-time high in 40 years in 2016. This is undoubtedly a spiritual battle at so many levels.

I am of the belief we are nearing the gate of a final frontier. We will begin to see this nation and other nations in the world, move from regretting the past to a radical perspective of an amazing future. Please note: I'm not denying the fact that unwelcomed choices of the past can serve as a learning curve in life. **But who says we must carry them for the rest of our life as some sort of punishable reminder of what we wish we would've, could've done.**

In conjunction with some wonderful spiritual truths, I have incorporated some amazing scientific discoveries on how memories actually work and the ability we have to eradicate them. In addition, I will unlock the eternal mysteries of heaven; and include some spiritual exercises on how to erase hurtful emotions from the past. This is not an attempt to merely help you survive or cope with unwanted circumstances from the past, but to help you bring them under your feet. In such a way, they lose all governing power over you. Personally, I have never liked the word "cope." It implies that someone is just getting by, or at best living in survival mode.

As sons and daughters of God, we are not here to just cope with the circumstances of life, but to transform them into a kingdom reality of heaven on Earth.

Many books have been written on how to remember. The list of "memory books" is seemingly endless. Even my book, *Total Recall, Remembering the Original You*, was written to teach and encourage people how to remember the original intent of God for their life. Yet, how many books have you read that teach you how to forget, specifically, unwanted memories? I believe there is a supernatural and natural side to most everything in life. Therefore, I have incorporated both perspectives in this book.

> *"Every good thing given, and every perfect gift is from above, coming down from the Father of lights, with whom there is no variation or shifting shadow."*
> *(James 1:17)*

Just one intractable and unwelcome memory can influence a lifetime of future perceptions, emotions and behavior, despite the greatest therapeutic efforts. As a result, countless people spend an entire lifetime trying to forget the misfortune of past years. The spiritual and scientific study of memory has many facets to its function in life. Most people believe forgetting memories, whether of bad experiences or poor choices, are not an option. Many are convinced their only choice is to just live with the painful experiences of the past.

I am fully convinced, and I am living proof, that it is a powerful probability to reformat the former years of our life, in such a manner, that the goodness of God will override the past with his prevailing love and kindness. I believe anyone can have a hopeful desire to not only forget their ill choices of former years, but to also erase them as if they never happened.

One of the primary keys to forgetting is in the realm of emotion. Emotions link to visual reminders that haunt people for a lifetime. Evil attempts to devalue the human race by convincing the individual, they are nothing more than a statistical process of life that is easily replaced by the next person in line. This kind of thinking can send most people down a depressed road that has no end.

In more ways than one, it seems our greatest advantage to encountering the future is learning how to forget the past.

In **Philippians 3:13,** Paul writes,

"Brethren, I do not regard myself as having laid hold of it yet; (the full perfection of Christ) but one thing I do; forgetting what lies behind and reaching forward to what lies ahead."

Paul seems to be saying, in order for us to obtain to the highest possible mark in Christ; we need to forsake, thus leave behind the ill choices of the past. Though we might never really know the full extent of regrets in Paul's life, it's probable his former actions of sentencing followers of Jesus to death were at the top of his regrets. After his conversion, the enemy undoubtedly tormented Paul (then named Saul) with his actions as a former Roman soldier. I believe his previous commands of persecuting Christians, in conjunction with having them stoned to death, became an eventual torment in his life.

Though there were circumstances in my past life that brought out the worse in me, I now have no sense of any real memorable emotion or connection to any of it. It's as though the memories were attached to another person that no longer exists, and when he died, the memories died with him. While drowning in my once regretful state, I managed to squelch numerous opportunities that would have afforded me a much richer life of peace, joy and prosperity.

Once God brought me into a deeper revelation of his love and forgiveness everything quickly began to change. I entered into an eventual understanding of not only how to be free from unwanted mistakes and experiences, but how to completely erase the images and emotional impact from my heart and mind. It was as if they had never happened. Forgetting what lies behind is instrumental to our future progression in life. This includes all the regrettable choices for pleasures that might have branded our hearts with eventual disappointment. **Forgetting the past is not always related to hurt and pain, but to pleasurable moments that cunningly attach themselves to the soul, thus creating a disaster for future relationships.**

For me, overcoming the past came through an intense revelation of God's word, as well as, learning how to supernaturally engage with the kingdom of heaven. As you might well know, overcoming the past can feel like an ongoing harassment of "now you see me, now you don't."

However, let me assure you, you can break free from the cycle of continual reminders that often try to depreciate God's intense love for you.

King David wrote,

> *"I will praise You, for I am fearfully and wonderfully*
> *made; marvelous are Your works, and that*
> *my soul knows very well."*
> *(Psalms 139:14)*

It is my hope you will freshly discover how fearfully and wonderfully made you are, and for the marvelous works of God to become evident in the deepest chambers of your heart and mind. You will soon discover there are multiple pathways leading to a welcomed perception of past events, all of which have the potential to set you on a course to complete healing and freedom from unwanted memories.

The Psalmist David writes,

> **"You see, God takes all our crimes, all our seemingly**
> **inexhaustible sins and removes them. As far as the east**
> **is from the west, He removes them from us."**
> **(Psalms 103:12... The Voice TNT)**

Unlike the North and South Pole, there is no place at which east and west meet. If David had said, "As far as the north is from the south" then that would imply, at some point, we would eventually meet up with our past sins again. I love this. It's like sealing the door to the darkness of the past with a permanent weld of his love. You have probably heard the saying, "It's nothing that time can't heal." While time does have the ability to distance someone from their past, it doesn't have the power to erase emotional trauma or unwanted memories. Most people just tuck away unwanted memories somewhere in the back of their mind, hoping they eventually disappear.

In light of the above scripture, it seems David had a profound experience and revelation of having the sins and failures of the past removed from his life.

When God, through Jesus, removed unrighteousness from our life, he literally moved it out of the record of time and space. He didn't just push our sins somewhere back into the distant past; he literally removed them as if they never even happened.

Once the past is under the blood of Jesus, forgetting the past is not an issue with God, but with us. Leaving the past behind still requires our refusal to entertain the ugliness of our past, keeping it out of the consciousness of our mind. Is this really possible? Yes, it is. No matter the intensity of pain or regret that you might have experienced in the former years of your life, through Christ, you have the power to remove it as though it never happened. **Close the door to your past and it will have no access to your future.**

Another powerful scripture that supports this understanding and has been transformative in my life is found in the book of Hebrews.

"I will be merciful when they fail,
I will erase their sins and wicked acts out of My
memory as though they had never existed."
(Hebrews 8:12...The Voice TNT)

Wow! Every time I think on this passage of scripture, waves of glory run up and down my spine. I've had heavenly encounters when the Lord would invite me to come and lie down on the altar of mercy and grace. At, which time, I would experience a loving adjustment in the glory realm. When I first read this scripture I thought, "If God can erase my sins and wicked acts out of his memory, why can't I do the same?" The Hebrew word "erase" means to abolish, to obliterate. It means to literally obliterate the memory from under heaven. Again, it's important that you catch this.

Anything and everything under heaven is subject to everything in heaven.

Imagine the love of God like some giant eraser reaching into the chalkboard of your heart and literally erasing away any and every emotional trauma or ill regret from your consciousness. You see, the heart is the center of your mind, not the brain. We actually think from our heart and then our brain stores it away like an internal hard drive.

Once a memory is erased from the heart, which is the seat of our emotions, it will eventually fade away from the hard drive of our life.

> *"For as a man thinks (reckons) within himself,*
> *so he is…"*
> *(Proverbs 23:7)*

Supernatural Reset #1

Close your eyes and imagine every painful regret and unwanted experience in your life written on the chalkboard of your heart.

Now imagine the hand of God reaching into your heart with a glorious eraser, stained with the blood of Jesus.

See him erasing away every unwanted regret, trauma, or any other wound in your heart.

Now see the hand of God writing on your heart his love plan for your life.

And at the conclusion, see Jesus leaving his signature on your heart that reads, "Eternally yours, Jesus."

Now write down every experience you saw the hand of God erasing from your heart and mind.

_____

_____

_____

_____

_____

_____

_____

_____

_____

_____

_____

_____

_____

Chapter 2

Lenses of Love, Forgiveness and Gratitude

When Jesus was on earth he was fully aware of his purpose in life; to override the law of sin and death, bringing mankind into the revelation of sonship, giving us full access to the kingdom of heaven. Jesus chose to deal with the cross by redirecting his emotions away from death to life. I believe Jesus directed his emotions through the eyes of love. Jesus undoubtedly had moments of intense conflict in the garden, knowing he was going to the cross to die a horrible death. Therefore, Jesus had to make a conscious emotional shift in his life.

Jesus redirected his focus and emotions from the dread of the cross to the "joy that was set before him."

The Bible declares,

> *"Looking to Jesus, the author and perfecter of faith, who for <u>the joy set before Him</u> endured the cross, despising the shame, and has sat down at the right hand of the throne of God."*
> *(Hebrews 12:1-2)*

The Voice translation reads like this,

> *"Now stay focused on Jesus, who designed and perfected our faith. He endured the cross and ignored the shame of that death because <u>He focused on the joy that was set before Him</u>; and now He is seated beside God on the throne, a place of honor."*

Jesus walked in the revelation of directing his thoughts to the greater good. The power of endurance came through Jesus's ability to see beyond the present day into the joy set before him. What Jesus saw was literally right in front of him, beyond space and time.

The blood Jesus bled in the garden wasn't just from the anguish or fear of dying a painful death, as horrible as that was. It was also the horror of the Son of God being identified with the "shame of death" which creates a perception of being guilty of wrongdoing, thus labeled a sinner. Shame is the consequence of sin, thus the association to guilt. Yet, we know Jesus knew no sin.

"He made Him who knew no sin to be sin on our behalf, so that we might become the righteousness of God in Him."
(2 Corinthians 5:21)

Many have mistaken this passage of scripture to say that Jesus became sin on our behalf. However, I believe a more accurate understanding is Jesus was portrayed as a sinful person, when in fact he was not guilty or *"knew no sin."* As intense as all of this was, Jesus ignored the image of shame, because of the joyous result of his obedience to the Father.

Seeing into the future joy of what was to come was no small thing. He could see his own eternal glorious state, as well as, the glory of future sons and daughters of God. In this same sense, forgetting the influences of your past hinges on your ability to emotionally disconnect from images and experiences that portray you as something less than you really are.

To the degree you are able to set your eyes on your new creative state in the kingdom of God is the degree you will be able to see beyond the lying shame of the past.

The two keys to forgetting the past and locking on to the future is seeing the past through the eyes of **love** and **joy**. Depending on your circumstances, seeing the past through the love and joy of the Father might seem very challenging. Responding with love and joy doesn't mean you are happy about the darkness of the past. However, it does provide you with the opportunity to filter those unwanted memories through the lenses of love and joy,

19

thus removing their demeaning effect from your life. The love and joy of the Lord will supernaturally give you the strength to move beyond the clutches of any unwanted experience in your life.

> *"...the joy of the Lord is your strength!"*
> *(Nehemiah 8:10)*

> *"...for love covers a multitude of sins."*
> *(1Peter 4:8)*

Love covering a multitude of sin does not imply sweeping bad stuff under the rug; it is far more meaningful that. The Hebrew word "love" is "kaphar." It means to cover up. It is often translated as "atonement." Atonement is an outward action that covers over an error in life as though it never happened. It also means, to prevent disclosure or recognition of any sinful act. It means to completely remove it from sight. It also means to remove it from the sight of your mind as well. Its intent is to provide protection and security from any harmful action. Wow!

Supernatural Reset #2

Here is a simple process for disconnecting from former actions or circumstances that might try to lock you in an image of guilt and shame.

Disconnect from any former shame by setting your sights on your current position in Jesus Christ.

Know that anything that tries to frame you in a life that is less than pure righteousness is a lie.

You are not a by-product of former guilt, but of love and forgiveness.

Anything that tries to lock you into a mind that is less than royalty is not from God.

Now, write down a glorious royal reaction to each past unwanted encounter God has removed from your life. In other words, instead of shame, see your heavenly Father celebrating you as if you just made him the proudest Father ever.

_____

_____

_____

_____

_____

_____

_____

_____

_____

_____

_____

_____

_____

_____

_____

_____

_____

_____

_____

_____

Forgiveness

I can't think of a more appropriate way to override the darkness of the past than with forgiveness. Without forgiveness, trying to leave the past behind is literally impossible. While this subject is worthy of an entire book, which others have already written, I am still compelled to somewhat expound on this amazing truth. I believe forgiveness is the epicenter of God's love.

One of Jesus's most intense declarations came through a very dark agonizing moment in his life. After being whipped and brutally nailed to a wooden cross, in his final hour of death, he declared,

> *"Father! Forgive them for they do not know*
> *what they are doing."*
> *(Luke 23:34)*

This is one of the most powerful acts of love anyone could ever express. Through every regrettable moment in your life those words of forgiveness were continually being herald over you. In your worst state, God held you in his heart and purposed to love you through every challenging moment of your life. This eternal revelation is vital to anyone's progression in life. Like an internal sword of truth, the power of forgiveness has the power to pierce into the deepest parts of our being. Jesus knew the power of forgiveness and its ability to overcome all the works of the enemy. As our glorious divine leader, he set the bar of love at the highest level.

John quotes Jesus as saying,

"Now judgment comes upon this world and everything will change. The tyrant of this world, satan, will be thrown out. When I am lifted up from the earth, then all of humanity will be drawn to Me."

"These words foreshadowed the nature of His death."
(John 12:31-33)

The moment Jesus was lifted upon the cross and then lifted up out of the grave of death, all of humanity has since been drawn toward the forgiveness of Jesus Christ. This same forgiveness was so great that it literally rendered satan, the tyrant of the world, powerless. This is what the power of forgiveness can do in your life. It can literally cast every hurtful and demeaning experience of your past into the sea of forgetfulness. Overshadowing you with the divine nature of the forgiving love of Jesus.

Those same words of forgiveness have continued to echo throughout the ages. They are a constant reminder of the intensity of God's love for all humanity. I believe forgiveness is the primary path to living a victorious life from any unwanted memory of the past. From a Hebraic perspective, forgiveness means, **"to overlook an offense and treat the offender as not guilty."**

This is the "overshadowing" that John was referring to in the previous verse in *John 12:33*. It is the shadow of forgiveness. The power of love overlooks an offense and treats the offender as not guilty.

King Solomon described it like this,

"He has brought me to his banquet hall,
And his banner over me is love."
(Song 2:4)

I prophesy this over your life right now,

"Whatever your regretful act might have been, whether it
was for pleasure or pain that had a negative impact in
your life, Jesus overshadows you with these amazing
words, "You Are Forgiven!"

His banner over you is love! Any guilt or shame you are
still experiencing from your past is not coming from your
heavenly Father, but from the father of lies.

Let these words forever be branded in your heart.

"Therefore, there is now no condemnation for
those who are in Christ Jesus."
(Romans 8:1)

Wow! Come on God!

In order to fully access this overshadowing grace in your
life, you have to overshadow others with the same grace
and forgiveness.

"For If you forgive others for their transgressions, your
heavenly Father will also forgive you."
(Mathew 6:14)

Of course, from a natural perspective, this might seem
impossible; depending on the intensity of hurt and pain
in your life. Nonetheless, without forgiveness, your
desire to be emotionally free from past experiences will
be next to impossible. As I already stated before, there
are many undesirable memories that are not necessarily
connected to pain. Former choices of pleasure attach

themselves to the soul, thus become a potential hazardous gateway for future relationships. Therefore, releasing the power of forgiveness over yourself will ensure your ability to walk free of any and all regrets in your life.

When I say, "free" I mean as free as if it never happened. This is the power of love and grace given to you by the Holy Spirit. Seeing yourself fully clothed in the righteousness of Jesus Christ will always afford you the glorious privilege of seeing your new creative state in Him.

Paul writes,

"Therefore, if anyone is in Christ, he is a new creature; the old things passed away; behold, new things have come."
(2Cor 5:17)

"I have been crucified with Christ; and it is no longer I who live, but Christ lives in me; and the life which I now live in the flesh I live by faith in the Son of God, who loved me and gave Himself up for me."
(Galatians 2:20)

Supernatural Reset #3

I declare you are in Christ. You are in union with the Anointed One. Therefore, you have literally been transformed into a new creation, which means you are framed and formed out of a fresh quality of character that is born directly out of the heart of God.

The past actions of your life, which were once archaic and primitive, have been consumed by God's everlasting love and desire toward you. As a result, you have entered into a new existence in the kingdom of God. You are redeemed!

Now write down your own personal declaration of God's redemptive power working in your life. For example, Declare, "I am redeemed by the blood of the Lamb!"

_____

_____

_____

_____

_____

_____

_____

_____

_____

_____

_____

_____

_____

_____

_____

_____

_____

_____

_____

_____

_____

Forgetting the Past Through a Thankful-Grateful Heart

There are a lot of books written on the subject of having a heart of thankfulness and gratitude. I want to do so again but present them as a key to forgetting unwanted memories. Years ago, in my early twenties, I had a terrifying experience with a drug ringleader. Even as I speak about it now, it's as though it happened a thousand years ago. While I have no current emotional impact from that memory, I can vaguely remember another man (which was me) wanting to end this person's life.

Almost ten years later, I had an amazing God encounter. Shortly thereafter this man whom I hated so much, came to my mind. I knew the Lord was dealing with my heart. Knowing I was dealing with an unforgiving heart, I inquired of the Lord, how to be rid of this horrible memory. I distinctly remember the Lord saying, **"Forgive him with a heart of thanksgiving and release blessings upon his life."**

Without hesitation I began to forgive him and gave thanks to the Lord for his life and God's plan to redeem him, just as he redeemed me. Every time the darkness of that day tried to resurface in my life, I would release the blessings of God over that situation, until one day, the haunting memories of that moment completely faded away, never to return.

I have since learned, a thousand times over, taking the time to be thankful and appreciative for things you have received, tangible or intangible, makes you emotionally more positive and causes you to relish good experiences. It also helps improve your health, helps deal with adversity, and builds strong relationships. So how does this thankful gratitude help someone to forget unwanted memories? First, while thankfulness and gratitude are in the same family of intent, their meanings slightly differ from one another. Gratitude is defined as, "the quality of being thankful, which reveals a readiness to show appreciation for something through returned kindness." Thankfulness is defined as, "being pleased or relieved. It's an emotion of gladness that is expressed when something has happened or not happened."

Gratitude is expressed by doing something in return for what was given. Whereas, thankfulness is more of an emotional response to what was received or experienced. These two expressions undoubtedly form a great marriage and are uniquely effective in overriding any unwanted memories. This does not minimize the fact that painful memories are very real, but it does place them within the perspective of eternity, thus lessening their impact in the light of God's love.

The Psalmist David writes,

> *"Give thanks to the Lord, for He is good,*
> *For His lovingkindness is everlasting.*
> *Give thanks to the God of gods,*
> *For His lovingkindness is everlasting.*
> *Give thanks to the Lord of lords,*
> *For His lovingkindness is everlasting."*
> *(Psalms 136:1-3)*

The Hebrew word for "thanks" is "yawd." It refers to **"an open hand"** as in the open hand of God. It signifies that God's power, means, and direction is readily available to whoever asks for it. These three ingredients of God's open hand are powerful enough to take all the poor choices and experiences in our past and turn them into a glorious perspective of what is to come.

A study done with undergraduate students in 2014 revealed the effects of Thanksgiving on a person's well-being over a very short period of time. It was reported that these students had higher levels of positive emotions on the Thanksgiving holiday than any other days of the study. When these same researchers took a deeper look at what differentiated those who felt positive emotions on Thanksgiving from those who didn't, they found that participants who expressed gratitude and thankfulness on that day were more likely to feel positive emotions on Thanksgiving and increased "life satisfaction" on the coming days. In addition, other research examined how counting your blessings impacts overall well-being, which reminds me of the lyrics of an old hymn I used to sing in church.

"Count your blessings; name them one by one
Count your blessings; see what God has done
Count your blessings; name them one by one
Count your blessings and see what God has done."

Further studies have proved that most successful business minds discuss the importance of living a gratitude-filled life. It was noted in 2014, Mark Zuckerberg challenged himself to write one thank-you note a day to counter his critical nature and express more gratitude, which he says, "highly affected the outcome of his life." Billionaire investor Warren Buffett has often given credit to a grateful heart for his high level of achievements in the stock market. G.K. Chesterton, an English writer, poet, philosopher, dramatist, journalist, orator and lay theologian writes, "I would maintain that thanks are the highest form of thought, and that gratitude is happiness doubled by wonder."

The Apostle Paul writes,

> *"In everything give thanks; for this is God's*
> *will for you in Christ Jesus."*
> *(1 Thessalonians 5:18)*

He is not saying we should give thanks for everything, but *"to give thanks in everything."*

In this sense we know,

> **"God causes all things to work together for good to**
> **those who love God, to those who are called**
> **according to His purpose."**
> **(Romans 8:28)**

Out of all the famous books in the Bible, the book of Psalms is the most thankful and grateful book ever written. In its pages are countless, wondrous keys to forgetting unwanted memories.

Supernatural Reset #4

Let me encourage you to read the following scriptures in such a way that you envision every unwanted memory drowning beneath their glorious intent of heaven for your life.

These are only but a few thankful and grateful passages that will undoubtedly lead you into a glorious perspective of who you are in the Father's heart, thus eradicating every unwanted memory, as though they never were.

"I will give thanks to the Lord with all my heart;
I will tell of all your wonders."
(Psalms 9:1)

"I will give thanks to the Lord according to His
righteousness and will sing praise to the
name of the Lord Most High."
(Psalms 7:17)

"That my soul may sing praise to you and not be silent.
O Lord my God, I will give thanks to You forever."
(Psalms 30:12)

"I will give you thanks in the great congregation; I will
praise you among a mighty throng."
(Psalms 35:18)

"I will give thanks to You, O Lord, among the peoples;
I will sing praises to you among the nations."
(Psalms 57:9)

"I will give thanks to You, O Lord my God, with all my
heart, and will glorify Your name forever."
(Psalms 86:12)

For scriptures that come to your heart.

_____
_____
_____
_____
_____
_____
_____
_____
_____
_____
_____
_____
_____
_____
_____
_____
_____
_____
_____
_____
_____
_____
_____
_____

Chapter 3

Traveling Through Time

Many know all too well the memories they want to hang on to and the memories they don't will often mingle together. The idea of pulling them apart seems like an impossible task. I've had the misfortune of knowing first-hand what this is like.

In August of 2014, I found myself pacing back and forth on a cold concrete hospital floor, just outside the operating room where they were performing emergency surgery on my wife Lori. My mind was frantically racing from one thought to the next trying to lock into the reality of what had just happen. Lori was having a major heart attack and was now fighting for her life. Still in disbelief, we were all trying to reel in the sudden crisis at hand. It appeared as though Lori was getting stronger, then in the last few days she suddenly took a turn for the worst.

Finally, after what seemed like a lifetime of waiting the surgeon called the family together. He began to carefully walk us through the procedures of the last few hours, which at first, gave us a sense the worst was now over. Yet, I knew in my heart something went terribly wrong.

Interrupting the surgeon, I said, "What are you trying to say?"

He stopped, looked at me and said, "I'm sorry, we tried everything we could, but could not bring her back."

Like a dark stormy cloud, his words came crashing down over me. I had thought the previous heavenly encounters I had shared with Lori just a few days prior, were a sure sign of restoration.

As I stood there, trying to sort through the impact of the surgeon's words, he said, "I know you are a minister, so I think you will appreciate what I am about to tell you." Giving me a moment to collect my thoughts, he said, "After your wife was pronounced dead, a few moments later, she pulled her hand out of the hand of the nurse standing beside her and lifted her arms into the air. It was as if she was reaching up to someone." He then added, "I knew this was an intentional response and not just some involuntary reaction of a lifeless body."

I had no doubt that Jesus or an angel had come to escort Lori to heaven. I will never forget the intensity of peace and assurance that came over me after hearing those words. I knew Lori was right where she wanted to be.

I was escorted to the operating room where Lori's body was still lying on the operating table. As I sat down on a chair beside her, Sheryl, my sister in-love, came and sat down beside me. We both sat there staring at Lori's lifeless body. As my eyes blurred with tears, I wanted to make some bold command like, "I rebuke this spirit of death! Rise up in Jesus name!" But all I could hear were the words Lori spoke to me a couple of months prior to this moment.

She said, "Michael, I'm ready to go to heaven." It made me very angry. I knew she was just saying it because she felt like she was being a burden to me.

"Don't buy into that lie!" I shouted. "Continuing this journey without you is not an option!"

I will never forget the soberness on her face when she said, "Michael, I'm not giving up, but promise me, if something goes wrong, you won't try to bring me back."

"I quickly turned away and said, "I'm done with this conversation. You're going to be fine."

As I sat there staring at her lifeless form, contrary to her wishes, I still managed to speak out a lame rebuke, commanding her spirit to come back into her body. Yet, Sheryl and I both knew Lori was not coming back to this feeble body ever again.

Shortly after, my brother Craig came and stood beside me. I cried on his broad shoulders. Though we knew Lori was no longer there, we said our last goodbyes and then returned to comfort the rest of the family.

Rewritten – Editing Futures Past

After Lori's graduation into heaven, I searched through my mind for all the possible choices that might have turned this painful outcome around. Yet, every scenario ended up at the same door. Lori was gone, and she wasn't coming back, well, at least not outside her renewed state in the kingdom of God. After 36 years of marriage, I never thought I would one day be staring up at my bedroom ceiling trying to entertain a future without her.

I would like to share the heavenly encounter I shared with Lori just a few days prior to her going into the hospital. At the time, I thought for sure it would free her from any roadblock to divine healing. My supernatural experience was literally like the old Charles Dickens *Ghost-Story of Christmas,* commonly known as, *A Christmas Carol.*

It's the story of Ebenezer Scrooge, an old miser who is visited by the ghost of his former business partner Jacob Marley and the Ghosts of Christmas Past, Present and Yet to Come. After their visits Scrooge is transformed into a kinder, gentler man. In a similar way, this was my experience. Except, I like to think I am much kinder than the scrooge in Dickens's story. In much the same way, God took me into the recorded past of my life. I literally relived early experiences in Lori's and my marriage.

I was shown how some of my previous actions and words had deeply wounded Lori's heart for a great number of years. I could literally see the scars I had created in her life laying in the deepest chambers of her soul. On each occasion, God gave me the opportunity to override some hurtful moments in Lori's life with an intense love, honor and affection.

I had said some things to Lori that were very demeaning, unknowingly depreciating her worth as a mother, wife and daughter of God. The ugliness of my words cut me to the core. I was horrified at how hateful my words sounded and the impact they had on Lori's heart. My whole body shook with tears as I cried out to the Lord for forgiveness. In that same instant, the Spirit invited me to reconstruct those horrendous moments with words of honor and glory.

After each occurrence, I hugged Lori tightly and kissing her on the forehead, I said, "You are beautiful, and I bless you with an everlasting love."

After each encounter, her countenance miraculously changed. I could visibly see her being crowned with the love and joy of the Lord. I then cried with overwhelming joy. As this divine moment neared its end, I felt the healing virtue of the Lord rising up in Lori's heart and mine.

It was one of the most intense cleansings I had ever encountered. It reminded me of my initial love encounter with Jesus when I had fully yielded my life to him many years back. A thousand pounds fell off me. I then saw Lori ascend into the throne room of heaven and vanish from my sight. Upon my return home, I shared all the details of my encounters with her and with tears streaming down her face and mine, she said, "I love you Michael. I feel such an amazing presence of God's love." We both cried tears of joy.

As you can imagine, I had perceived all of this as an amazing opportunity for Lori to receive healing in her heart and body. Little did I know that two days later, Lori would literally be lifted up into the throne room of heaven, into the arms of Jesus.

I realize now that it was the grace and mercy of God working in both our lives. Lori's sudden departure could have potentially left me with some intense regrets. Yet, God, in all his goodness and mercy brought healing to us both. I will forever be grateful. While all this might seem too impossible to be true by faith, you too, can travel through time, into a moment in history where God will afford you the opportunity to rewrite the past.

Supernatural Reset #5

You too, can release blessings over any past experience that the enemy has tried to use against you or someone close to your heart.

Whatever those past moments might have been, all you need to do is see yourself overriding every demeaning word or action with words of love, glory and honor.

Once you have done this, let me challenge you to seal the moment however your heart directs you. For me, it was the kiss of life, which was nothing less than the kiss of God's love and supernatural healing.

Don't be afraid to repeat this process as often as you feel led to by the Spirit.

Don't ever let the enemy cheat you out of an amazing opportunity to bring healing to your heart and those around you.

_____

_____

_____

_____

_____

_____

_____

_____

_____

_____

Time Travel for Dummies

I realize the whole "rewriting the past" thing can be a bit challenging, especially, if you come from a more conservative background. As for me, my conservative Southern Baptist up bringing offered me very little room for such possibilities. This is certainly no fault of my parents, like those before them; they did not have a revelation of their greater potential as sons and daughters of God.

Sometime ago, I walked up to the podium at Glory Fire Church in Sanford, Florida. I humorously began with these words, "Tonight, we are going to begin our session with *Time Travel for Dummies.*" Before you conclude that I was calling everyone stupid, let me clarify this statement.

According to Mr. Merriam-Webster,

"A dummy is something designed to resemble and serve as a substitute for the real or usual thing."

In other words, a dummy can be an obscured version of the real deal. The apostle Paul might liken this to *1Corithians 13:12,*

"For now we see in a mirror dimly, but then face-to-face..."

In this sense, our dumbness is subjected to our level of understanding in any given moment. I believe time and space is a dumbed down version of eternal time and space. The first is temporary, while the later is eternal. Another way of saying it is the first is limited, while the later is limitless.

At the basic level most people travel through time every minute of every day, without even realizing it. In your mind, whenever you reflect on something in the past, present or future; you are subconsciously traveling through time and space. In this sense we are constantly traveling back and forth through time every second of every day.

This simple process of time travel intensely escalates at a very young age. As a result, we become less aware that we are traveling through time. In other words, over the years, we are constantly looking at something we did; we are doing or are going to do. So much so, we don't even realize we are actually traveling through time and space. As a result, we become dull to the fact that we are time travelers of another kind.

Yes, it is true; we are able to travel through time within the capsule of our own mind. In the same manner, we can travel in the spirit.

While this is certainly not an attempt to dumb down the supernatural reality of traveling in the spirit, it is an attempt to bring the basics of time travel within your reach. As I have already stated before, through the love of God, I was afforded the opportunity to override a wrong with a right. I realize how difficult it might be for any rational person to embrace such an extraordinary possibility. Nonetheless, my experience was as real as watching the rising of the morning sun. Over the last several years, I have come to understand the ability God has given to all of us to travel through the tenses of time, thus deal with any harmful intent.

I believe understanding the basics of time travel can greatly enhance our ability to deal with the past supernaturally. One of the first steps is realizing through the spirit, we are not governed by the laws of physics, which positions us to entertain the possibility of breaking the barrier of space-time.

I've often thought about Phillip who baptized a eunuch in the river and as they both came up out of the water, Phillip disappeared. *(Acts 8:26-40)*

Then there was the Jesus, a crowd of people became so angry with him they tried to push him off a cliff. When they did, Jesus supernaturally passed right through the crowd like an invisible ghost. *(Luke 4:28-30)*

Like Jesus, many of our unwanted and unexpected encounters have the potential to become divine opportunities, causing us to realize our full potential as sons and daughters of God.

As you can see, breaking the barrier of space-time is a normal way of life in the kingdom of God.

However, rest assure, even if you're not able to reconstruct unwanted experiences in your past in the way I have described, it's important to know the love of Jesus is still sufficient to cause all things to work together for the greater good in your life.

"And we know that God causes all things to work together for good to those who love God, to those who are called according to His purpose."
(Romans 8:28)

In the meantime, we must never forget that time and space is an elusive government that can easily be broken through faith.

In the Bible, Jesus is noted as saying; "The kingdom of God" or the "kingdom of heaven" is like this or that. Jesus masterfully used analogies of the natural realm to create pathways into the spirit.

To a Hebrew, the Bible is pictographic. Throughout New Testament scriptures, Jesus used pictographic analogies from Jewish culture as a point of reference to bring the people of that day into the kingdom of heaven.

Matthew writes,

"He told them another parable. The kingdom of heaven is like leaven that a woman took and hid in three measures of flour, till it was all leavened.

The kingdom of heaven is like a treasure hidden in the field, which a man found and hid again; and from joy over it he goes and sells all that he has and buys that field.

The kingdom of heaven is like a merchant in search of fine pearls, who, on finding one pearl of great value, went and sold all that he had and bought it."
(Matthew 13:44-46)

Through parables, Jesus created a bridge from the natural to the spirit. He created a supernatural portal that enabled those listening to travel from one dimension to another. Though they were not fully aware of their traveling experiences, through their divine imaginations, they were afforded the opportunity to engage with the kingdom of heaven.

Chapter 4

Directing Your Thoughts

Jennice Vilhauer, PhD, is the author of several books. She is director of the Adult Outpatient Psychotherapy Program and an assistant professor in the Department of Psychiatry and Behavioral Science in the School of Medicine at Emory University in Atlanta, Georgia. She is also the developer of Future Directed Therapy.

In her book, ***Thinking Forward to Thrive***, she writes,

"If you are experiencing emotional pain, it is because you are thinking about the unwanted aspects of a situation. Many people feel they have to resolve painful or difficult issues, and for that reason they spend too much time thinking about things that do not make them feel good.

Some people feel that when they redirect their thoughts, they are simply distracting themselves or avoiding the issue. However, redirecting your thinking constructively is not the same as avoidance; in fact, it is one of the most positive coping strategies that you can develop!

While there are times when looking back at an unpleasant event to figure out how it could have gone better or how you could do it differently in the future is very useful, allowing yourself to ruminate on painful events can cause significant distress." (Jennice Vilhauer, PhD)

I love the idea of being the directors of our lives. I am not saying the spirit of God is not leading us, but the decision to follow the leading of his spirit is still ours to make. This kind of directive thinking requires a certain attitude.

Philippians 2:5 reads,

> *"Have this attitude in yourselves which was also in Christ Jesus..."*

Another translation reads,

> *"Let this mind be in you which was also in Christ Jesus..." (NKV)*

One of the primary directives for acquiring the mind of Christ is to **let** the same mind that is in Christ, be in us. "One of the key words here is **"let." In this sense, it means to make room for the greater intent of God for your life.** The Greek word "mind or attitude" means to "think, judge, observe or direct your mind to something."

Therefore, through Christ, we have the power to direct our own mind and thoughts in any particular direction. When your mind starts wandering to the darkness of your past, you have the power to redirect it toward the expectations of the future promises of God for your life.

At first, this process can be challenging, but once you practice this in your life you will enter into an amazing awareness of a renewed mind. With the mind of Christ, we have the ability to judge or observe something from a supernatural perspective. This is wonderful news for anyone who desires to forget previous sinful or painful actions of the past. It means, like God, we have the ability to literally erase any dark actions from our memory. Wow! Seriously? Come on God.

Superimposing the Past

In **Phil 3:13**, the word *"forget"* in this particular text means *"to lose out of mind, time, place and order."* Its implications are to transpose the landscape of your thinking into an entirely new image, place and time. It's the reconstruction of your thoughts. This same word also means to superimpose, as in the process of placing one image over another. In terms of forgetting the past, superimposition is the act of taking the opposite of one thing and placing it over another. "Inner healing" is another known term for this process.

While there are multiple ways to approach inner healing, a more common practice is through showing someone how to overlay hurtful events with images of Jesus's love, goodness and kindness.

I want to share an unexpected superimposition that occurred in my life, prior to Tamera and I reuniting. Heavenly visualizations have often played a key role for me in moving beyond past traumas in my life. During the first couple of months after Lori's heavenly graduation, I kept having flashbacks of seeing her lifeless body lying on a surgical table. Even while sleeping, I would wake up crying with the surgeon's words echoing in my ears, "I'm sorry, we tried everything we could, but could not bring her back."

Shortly thereafter, while doing some work in my office, I began to struggle with the future. The idea of planning out my life seemed virtually impossible. It felt as though the weight of the entire world was upon my shoulders. Every hopeful perspective seemed light years away. I had no more tears to cry. I was emotionally dried up. It was during this dryness in my life when I had an open vision of Jesus standing before me.

His smile was like the morning sun freshly shinning on me. All of the hopelessness in my heart was suddenly overcome with an enormous expectation for the future. As he reached out and put his hand over my heart, he said, "Michael, it's time to move on. Your journey is not over. The plans I have for you have only just begun." The look on his face and the sound of his words superimposed themselves over my heart. My heart and mind were literally overlaid with an intense hope that seemed to stretch beyond space and time.

In this same vision, when I looked over the right shoulder of Jesus; I could see Lori in the distance laughing. I knew she couldn't see me, but I could see her. Towering over her was a huge angel who seemed humorously entertained by their conversation. Lori certainly had a way of making you laugh. Suddenly my attention quickly shifted to a little boy holding Lori's hand. With a stunned realization, I knew he was our son. When Lori and I were much younger she became pregnant. Being the selfish person, I was at the time, I pressured her into getting an abortion. I later realized the deep pain I had brought into her life.

This was one of the scars I saw when God took me back in time, giving me the opportunity to speak blessings over Lori, thus rewriting a regretful decision in both our lives. It was a secret regret that we both carried in our hearts right up to her heavenly graduation. Now, seeing the joy on Lori's face and the smile of this little boy engaging with her and the angel became another enormous superimposition in my life. My heart was overlaid with an intense joy and memory of now giving birth to a son. I have a son! The imprint of that vision will forever be with me.

Once you release something over to the Lord, from his perspective, it's as though the regret of your past never happened.

Supernatural Reset #6

Allow God to superimpose his heart and mind over any undesirable memories in your life.

As horrible as those decisions might have been, see images of God's love coming down from heaven and overlaying any undesirable memories experience in your life.

Here is my decree over you right now:

"You are an amazing and powerful son/daughter of God. There is no end to the love that God has extended toward you in this time in your life.

Right now, God is inviting you into a moment of superimposition. He desires to overlay every part of your being with his eternal love and glory."

Through the blood of Jesus, the slate of your past has been wiped clean. Come on God!

_____

_____

_____

_____

_____

_____

_____

_____

_____

_____

Overriding Painful Emotions

At the moment of conception, emotions begin to escalate on all levels. Their influences increasingly play a major role in everyday life. They can either serve as fruitful experiences or they can become extremely painful, potentially imprisoning us into a world of lifelessness. ***Emotions were designed to serve humanity, not the other way around.*** When we become subservient to our emotions we yield ourselves to a field of government that strives to dictate our decisions at the most basic levels of living. Much of the scientific world believes if unwanted emotions from the past were removed, those same memories would lose their impact in our lives and simply disappear. **Emotions of previous experiences are what give power to the recorded images in our mind.**

In the context of unwanted memories, forgetting is defined as, **"becoming emotionally detached from unwanted experiences in the past."** This implies that forgetting and emotions go hand in hand.

Emotion is defined as,

"A mental state that arises spontaneously rather than through conscious effort and is often accompanied by physiological changes; a feeling, the emotions of joy, sorrow, and anger etc."

It's important to catch this thought. Emotions are not necessarily planned actions but are spontaneous responses that can arise at any given moment. For example: Suddenly, a past memory comes to mind and you spontaneously emotionally respond. Therefore, even your mental response was spontaneous. It's equally important to note that vulnerabilities of painful emotions often come through rehearsing the past. Every time you rehash your past, you emotionally relive it at one level or another.

The last thing you should be doing is sitting around revisiting unwanted memories of your old life with family or friends. Each time you do, you reopen a door, giving access to tormenting spirits in your life. This is not to say that at the beginning of your healing process you shouldn't revisit painful moments in order to receive healing and be rid of their injurious actions in your life. However, afterwards, there's no need to repeatedly go back and revisit (the old you) which in the eyes of God is dead, and never existed to begin with.

It's important to recognize you are no longer who you use to be. In other words, once you come into the realization of God's love for you, you are afforded the opportunity to discover the real you; the one made in the image and likeness of God. Even before you realized this amazing truth, you were already absolutely wonderful. So, if you are just now discovering this blessed reality about yourself, you should know you have always been beautiful in His sight.

Even if your choices in life might not have been the best, God still loved you so much that he gave his only Son for the purpose of restoring you to your original state in him. Yes, you are that amazing. Therefore, in order to destroy the emotional roots of your old nature, you must first be rejoined to your heavenly nature, which comes from above and not from below.

"We are partakers of his divine nature..."
(2Peter 1:4)

Once the love of God begins to take hold of your life, you will quickly come into alignment with the heart and mind of God, thus the bed of your emotions is renewed.

Paul writes,

"Do not be conformed to this world, but be transformed by the renewing of your mind, so that you may prove what the will of God is, that which is good and acceptable and perfect."
(Romans 12:2)

To the degree we relationally progress in God is the degree we can have God's perspective on what is good, acceptable and perfect. This supernatural improving is for all those he loves.

Paul writes again,

"I have been crucified with Christ; and it is no longer I who live, but Christ lives in me; and the life which I now live in the flesh I live by faith in the Son of God, who loved me and gave Himself up for me."
(Galatians 2:20)

I believe this is an important key to experiencing a complete overhaul in the emotional realm of our life. Being crucified with Christ means our old nature was put to death, along with all of its emotional baggage. If you have no recollection of ever dying to your old nature, thus being resurrected into life, then it would serve you well to attend your own funeral, which is the burial of the old you in Christ.

Supernatural Reset #7

Let me encourage you to read this aloud.

"Jesus, I believe when you died on the cross, because of your love for me, I died with you. Just as you were resurrected from the dead, so I have been resurrected from the dead works of my past, thus my old nature. Therefore, I declare this day, it is no longer I who lives, but Christ who lives in me."

Congratulations! If you prayed this prayer of faith, then you have engaged with the revelation of your first resurrection and have stepped into the endless realm of God's eternal love and promises for your life.

_____

_____

_____

_____

_____

_____

_____

_____

_____

_____

_____

_____

Chapter 5
Neurology and DNA

Reconstructing Memories

Many people know all too well that memories can feel like a bona-fide representation of the past. However, it has been scientifically proven that memories are constantly modified with new information. Therefore, most past events are reconstructed. The word "Reconstruct" is defined as, "to build or form something again after it has been damaged or destroyed. Other definitions of "reconstruct" are to rebuild, restore, renovate, recreate, remake, recondition and refurbish." In my case, God allowed me to reform my memories, thus removing any emotional damage from Lori's heart and mine by reconstructing previous experiences. According to the definitions above, this reconstruction process points to the ultimate restoration of all things.

*In **Acts** we read,*

"...He may send Jesus, the Christ appointed for you, whom heaven must receive until the period of restoration of all things about which God spoke by the mouth of His holy prophets from ancient time."
(Acts 3:20-21)

The Apostle Paul writes,

"For creation was subjected to futility, not of its own will, but because of Him who subjected it, in hope that the creation itself also will be set free from its slavery to corruption into the freedom of the glory of the children of God."
(Romans 8:20-21)

The power of restoration is part of our inheritance as sons and daughters of God. Hence, our ability to reconstruct the past and the future. You have probably heard of the analogy of a person sitting in a circle telling the first person a story, by the time it comes full circle the story line has completely changed with some added information. More often than not, it is the emotional mental perception of each individual that leads the story off of its original course of accuracy. One of the keys to preventing an increase of negative information about past experiences is through knowing how to sever any unwanted emotions related to each experience.

Over the last few years, a number of scientific discoveries have unveiled some very important information concerning the memory area of the brain and its capacity to forget. Neuroscientists have discovered each time you recall something, you reconstruct it, thereby making the memory of an event only as good as your recollection of it.

An interesting publication about reconstructing memories was posted in PYSBLOG, which is part of a scientific research group in the United Kingdom. **(Spring.org.uk)**

It tells a story about a young man named Sacks, who recalls a bomb falling on the streets of their city forcing them to take shelter with other people in their neighborhood. The story is detailed with emotions and experiences that would make you think young Sacks went through a horrific ordeal.

However, after further research they discovered something altogether different then what was told to them.

The article reads:

"When the autobiography of the once young man came out, one of his older brothers told him he'd misremembered the event. In fact, both of them had been at school when the bomb struck so they could not have witnessed the explosion.

The 'false' memory, it turned out, was implanted by a letter. Their elder brother had written to them, describing the frightening event, and this had lodged in his mind. Over the years the letter had gone from a third-person report to a first-person 'memory'.

Turning the memory over in his mind, Sacks writes that he still cannot see how the memory of the bomb exploding can be false. There is no difference between this memory and others he knows to be true; it felt like he was really there."

It is now a known fact that when memories are reconstructed, nerve cells in the brain produce proteins, which maintain the connection between the cells. However, it's not necessarily the memory in of itself that keeps the connection, but the emotion that it's attached to.

This means, every time the negative experiences of your past become a platform of conversation, they are reconstructed with new added information. This new information is added to the previous experience, thereby, creating an extended version of the original. As a result, you are reawakened to the emotion of a former experience, affording it another opportunity to influence your life in a negative manner.

Again, the question must be asked, is it really possible to erase unwanted memories from your mind? Given the variables of each individual life, it almost seems impossible to think we could actually erase, thus forget, the darkest episodes of earlier years. My life is a living example of what it is like to be impacted by intense trauma, and yet, watch it fade beneath the foundation of future promises and expectant hopes in the kingdom of God.

In conjunction with a supernatural approach to forgetting harmful memories (which we will get more into later in this book) I want to speak some more about the power of emotions and their relentless drive to keep us connected to negative experiences of the past. But before I do, I want to make one thing very clear, I am a firm believer,

"...that God causes all things to work together for good to those who love God, to those who are called according to His purpose."
(Romans 8:28)

No matter how hurtful some of those past things might have been in your life, once you bring them under the government of God's love they are immediately adjusted to serve the intentions of God for you. No matter how painful some of those things might have been in the former years of your life, in that state of darkness there is a hidden light that is destined to reveal the kingdom of God in your heart.

"The Light shines in the darkness, and the darkness did not comprehend it."
(John 1:5)

In other words, the light of God showed up in the darkest place and darkness didn't even see it coming, let alone understand its glorious intent. Let me expound on this subject a bit further. In my previous book, **Total Recall, How to Remember the Original You,** I wrote a chapter titled, *Memory in the Blood.* In this chapter I describe some scientific advances, and discoveries of how memories are carried over from one generation to the next through our DNA. For the benefit of those who have not read this particular book allow me to revisit a few things to catch you up to speed.

For most of my teenage years, I lived a very reckless life. I was always pushing things to the limit. In my hometown of Dryden, WA, you could always find me riding motorcycles, snowmobiles or any other vehicle with two or more wheels. Hardly a year would pass without my encountering some sort of accident, which usually resulted in broken bones, concussions or worse. Talk about a lapse in memory, it's truly a miracle that God has graced me with the physical stamina I have today.

Because of my wild years, in 1998 I was diagnosed as having formed a golf-ball sized cyst on the frontal lobe of my brain. This growth was the result of a number of concussions I had sustained years earlier. After the cyst was removed, I was anxious to move on beyond that traumatic period of my life. This meant I would no longer have to deal with focal seizures, which translated into knife jabbing pains behind my left knee.

Shortly after the surgery the seizures started up again. An enormous feeling of disappointment bombarded me, thinking this nightmare in my life was not over. I immediately called the neural surgeon wanting to know why I was still having these awful seizures.
I will never forget his reply.

He said, "Even though the cyst has been removed, your brain remembers the pain and is still acting as though you never had the surgery. Then he said, "Michael, it's very important that you stay in the mind that this cyst has been removed and the symptoms will subside in the near future."

Hearing those words sent a shock wave of revelatory relief throughout my body. In that moment, I made a decision not to take any more medication and stood in faith, believing that it was over. A short time later, the seizures stopped and never returned. I guess you might say it was a type of phantom limb pain, which is what a person feels after the loss of a limb.

At the most basic core of our being, memory is said to be in our blood. It is otherwise known as "cellular memory." Cellular memory is the hypothesis that such things as memories, habits, interests, and tastes are somehow stored in all the cells of our bodies.

On May 29, 1988, a woman named Claire Sylvia received the heart of an 18-year-old male who had been killed in a motorcycle accident. Soon after the operation, Sylvia noticed some distinct changes in her attitudes, habits, and tastes. She found herself acting more masculine, strutting down the street. Prior to Sylvia's heart transplant, she was an accomplished dancer. This meant that strutting like a man was not her normal posture. In addition, in this report, it was noted that she began to crave foods such as, green peppers and beer, which she had always disliked before.

Sylvia began having recurring dreams about a mystery man named Tim L. She had a strong feeling he was her donor. As it turns out, he was. When Sylvia met the family of her heart donor, she discovered that her donor's name was, in fact, Tim L. All the changes she had been experiencing in her attitudes, tastes, and habits closely mirrored that of Tim's. While some might find this a bit unnerving, maybe even spooky, I find it to be in perfect form with the design of God.

The memory of our natural state can often mirror the memory of our spirit. Memory of the spirit is in our blood. When Jesus shed his blood for mankind we received a heart transplant. Through this spiritual transfusion, like Sylvia, we supernaturally received the divine nature of God, thus his eternal memories and characteristics.

I want to make sure you are getting this.

Our DNA is filled with the mysteries of God's eternal nature. The blood of Jesus supernaturally flows through our veins. His redemptive power has made it so. Therefore, we have the ability to remember beyond this natural realm into the kingdom realms of heaven. In this sense, the blood of Jesus not only affords us the ability to remember former/eternal truths, but this same blood also empowers us to forget/erase unwanted memories as if they never happened.

Reconsolidating Your Brain

I spoke earlier about how memories are constantly modified with new information. Therefore, most past events are reconstructed to fit former recollections of each event. I would like to expound on the idea of erasing unwanted memories. Some years later after my first encounters with the light of God, increasing discoveries on "how to erase memories" quickly began to accelerate in the world of science.

On February 15, 2016, **Science Alert Magazine** printed this article titled,

"Scientists Know How to 'Erase' Your Painful Memories...And Add New Ones."

While this headline might sound a bit frightening to some, others who struggle with tormenting experiences from the past might find it a welcoming option. However, my goal is not to get you to pursue this as a method for forgetting the past, but to simply make you aware of the amazing breakthroughs that are now unfolding in the world of science.

Here is a quote from that report:

"How do you go about deleting a memory? To understand that, you need to understand how memories form and are kept alive in our brains. In the

past, scientists used to think that memories were stored in one specific spot, like a neurological file cabinet, but they've since realized that every single memory we have is locked up in a field of connections across the brain."

As already mentioned, the article goes on to explain how memory is formed when proteins stimulate our brains cells to grow and form new connections, literally rewiring our minds' circuitry. It describes how a memory is stored in our mind and when we repeatedly visit that memory, it will stay present in our mind. As I said before, revisiting the memory actually makes it unstable. Each time you do, it becomes stronger and stronger.

Science defines this process as **"reconsolidation."** Once you visit an unwanted memory enough times you reinforce it to the point where a mere thought can set off the emotion of that previous experience. The point of reconsolidation is where scientists have learned to hack memories. Apparently, memories can act as if they are in a molten state before becoming solid again. Every time a memory is revisited it becomes molten or jelled. At this stage the memory can be altered or "reconsolidated" before it resets itself. *When I look at all the above, my first thought is "Wow!" My second thought is "if this is true in the natural, how much truer is it in the spirit?"*

In *Total Recall, How To Remember The Original You*, I describe how the spirit of God; the blood of Jesus contains memory of who we are and who we were before time. At a cellular level, the DNA of Christ in us contains information of all life, past, present and future. This means the memory of our heavenly Father, through the blood of Jesus, was literally transferred into our being at a spiritual and cellular level.

It only makes sense that if the natural blood of humanity contains memory and can be handed down through the ages, how much more can the supernatural blood of Jesus contain memories before time.

In this sense, revelation is as much about remembering as it is discovering something new. It also means, the blood of Jesus in us has the ability to override any natural DNA. When it comes to forgetting unwanted memories, this is great news!

When you enter into the revelation of God's love, the renewing of your mind is subject to being reset according to the mind of Christ working in you.

Thus,

> *"...you are transformed by the*
> *renewing of your mind."*
> *(Romans 12:2)*

I know this is a repeat, but I want to make this very clear in a different way.

"While Jesus was hanging on the cross, he didn't just bleed into the ground, he bled into mankind, thereby redeeming humanity from a sinful nature."
(Mark Steen)

> *"We have obtained an inheritance, having been predestined according to His purpose who works all things after the counsel of His will..."*
> *(Ephesians 1:11)*

Supernatural Reset #8

Here is another very simple exercise to help you erase the pain of unwanted memories.

Again, please read aloud the following scriptures as a prophetic declaration over your heart and mind.

While doing so, envision the blood of Jesus, the eternal DNA of heaven flowing through your veins, which is nothing less than an eternal transfusion.

Then imagine every painful experience or regretful decision being washed away into the realm of no return.

Lastly, as you read these scriptures out loud, personalize them in your life.

> *"If we (I) walk in the Light as He Himself is in the Light, we have fellowship with one another, and the blood of Jesus His Son cleanses us (me) from all sin."*
> *(1 John 1:7)*

> *"I am in Christ, I am a new creature; old things have passed away; new things have come."*
> *(2 Corinthians 5:17)*

> *"I have been crucified with Christ; and it is no longer I who live, but Christ lives in me; and the life which I now live in the flesh I live by faith in the Son of God, who loved me and gave Himself up for me."*
> *(Galatians 2:20)*

Because of Christ, you are no longer who you used to be. Therefore, the decisions of your past have died with the old you and are no longer a part of the new you. Your future destiny has been reset according to the original intent of God for your life. Each time you meditate upon the word of God you will quickly discover the other you, the true you, the one born from above and not from below. As a result, you will take on the cellular memory of your original state in the heart of God, which was before the foundations of the world.

Sounds outrageous? It should, because that is just how amazing you really are.

_____

_____

_____

_____

_____

_____

_____

_____

_____

_____

Replacing the Old for the New

Another revelation as to how unwanted memories become a part of our lives is through "cellular impartation." If I haven't already made it clear, there are some natural aspects of our DNA that are very healthy and there are others that are not. This is true for both male and female. If I haven't already I want to make very clear that the blood of Jesus, the DNA of God is a redemptive glory that is powerful enough to override any earthly DNA that is contrary to the divine nature of heaven for our lives.

Nonetheless, knowing how to live in this redemptive realm of glory requires a renewing of the mind, which aligns itself with the mind of Christ.

There has been much debate over a study that was done at

the University of Seattle and the Fred Hutchinson Cancer Research Center, about women retaining and carrying living DNA from every man with whom they have sexual intercourse.

While many have debunked these findings, others still believe them to be accurate.

While both sides do agree that male and female can carry a level of foreign DNA in their bodies, they strongly differ as to the source of this DNA.

Nonetheless, I think we can all agree that after a man and woman connect through sexual intercourse, at one level or another, some bonding does indeed take place. Whether these times of intimacy are a one-night stand, or a more committal relationship in or outside of marriage, something is undoubtedly forged in their hearts and minds. At the very least, all the above have the potential of becoming a spiritual gateway into both lives.

Many have termed these types of interactions as "soul ties." While every situation carries its own unique circumstances, what if the brain could actually be decoded or recoded, both naturally and spiritually.

Decoding / Recoding of the Brain

Ever wonder how much memory your brain can actually store. Well, according to Scientific American (**scientificamerican.com**) while we might have only a few gigabytes of storage space, which is similar to the storage space in an iPod or a USB flash drive, the neurons in our brain combine in such a way that each one helps with countless memories at a time. Exponentially, this increases the **brain's memory** storage capacity to something much closer to 2.5 petabytes (or a million gigabytes). Throughout the scientific world, it's an agreed understanding that our brains are remarkable in their ability to encode and store an ongoing record of our life experiences. These encoded memories have an obvious impact in our life and have the ability to become the rudder of our purpose and destiny.

Since 2010, **PNAS (Proceedings of the National Academy of Sciences of the United States of America)** have successfully proven their ability to decode or recode the brain. For the sake of not wanting to drown us both in this deep scientific pool of how decoding and recoding of the brain works, in the most basic layman terms. Through a type of MRI imaging, known as "(fMRI) they now know how to detect individual memories through what is known as "neural decoding of memory states and past experiences."

This is just one of many other avenues the scientific world is currently pursuing with the hope of one day being able to download the memories of your past on to some form of storage device. Among other things, these same researchers believe these memory detection techniques will help them to conceivably interrogate the brains of suspected criminals or witnesses, who in the end will provide them with neural evidence of criminal activity.

I realize while this might seem fascinating to some, for others it's a bit unnerving.

With this seemingly impossible sci-fi revelation in mind, let's take another giant leap into the **supernatural** possibilities of decoding or recoding the brain.

Taking on the mind of Christ takes our capacity of memory to a whole new level. Forget the 2.5 petabytes (or a million gigabytes), with the mind of Christ, our memory capacity is infinite. In this sense "the renewal of our mind" is the process of decoding or recoding stored memories from an eternal heavenly perspective. As we grow up into the mind of Christ, we break the limitations of every physical process and storage of the human brain.

The Apostle Paul writes,

> *"For who has known the mind of the Lord, that he will instruct Him? But we have the mind of Christ."*
> *(1 Corinthians 2:16)*

Having the mind of Christ, in of itself is a decoder and recoder, all in one glorious package.

This means we can know what God is thinking.

The mind of Christ, who is the very image and likeness of God, is in us.

Again, Paul writes,

> *"And do not be conformed to this world, but be transformed by the* renewing *of your mind, so that you may prove what the will of God is, that which is good and acceptable and perfect."*
> *(Romans 12:2)*

The renewing of the mind is not simply a physical transformation of the brain; it is the renewing of the heart, which is the ultimate seat of our thinking, thus purposed to be centered in the mind of Christ.

> *"For as he (person) thinks in his heart, so is he..."*
> *(Proverbs 23:7)*

Therefore, the ultimate decoding (conversion) and recoding (a new state of being) of any unwanted memory in our life, comes through the revelation knowledge of who we are in him, and how we perceive ourselves in the light of his love.

Every record of our eternal state in God is in us now.

Therefore, through the power of the Holy Spirit every unwanted action from our past is decoded (converted) through the record of God's original intent for our life.

This means every memory has already been recoded (transformed) through the blood of Jesus.

Supernatural Reset # 9

I invite you to come boldly before the throne of grace and obtain mercy from God, at which time; he will release an assurance in your heart that he has already recoded (transferred) you from an earthly DNA signature to an eternal one.

Repeat after me:

"Every cell in my entire being has been conformed to the divine nature of God."

"I have been crucified with Christ; and it is no longer I who live, but Christ lives in me; and the life which I now live in the flesh I live by faith in the Son of God, who loved me and gave Himself up for me."
(Galatians 2:20)

Come on! Our God reigns and so do you!

_____
_____
_____
_____
_____
_____
_____
_____
_____
_____
_____
_____
_____
_____

Chapter 6
Beyond Earth

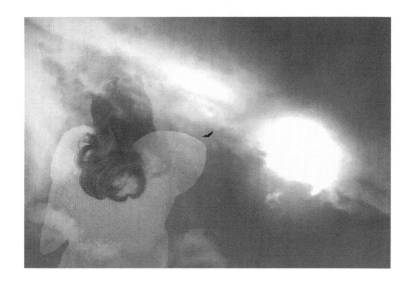

The River of Life

Sometime later, after Lori had graduated to heaven, I became reacquainted with my only high school sweetheart, Tamera. Other than a brief encounter at a church gathering in 2010 we had not seen each other in over 30 years.

Through multiple events, it eventually became apparent to us both that our moments of reconnecting were divinely orchestrated. During our brief courtship, Tamera expressed her desire to be emotionally healed of previous hurtful experiences in her past life.

One of the first encounters Tamera had in the kingdom of heaven was with the river of life. As described in Revelation 22, this river flows from the throne of God and has multiple pools along the way. I have encountered these pools many times. Here is a description of Tamera's experience with the river of God in her own words.

"On a Sunday in 2015, I wasn't feeling good, so I ended up watching a live stream of Michael speaking at MTI from home. Michael was teaching on how to forget unwanted experiences of the past. At the end of his message, he invited everyone to join him in a spiritual exercise.

I closed my eyes and listened as he led us into the river of life. I could see the river gently flowing past me with beautiful, friendly, welcoming waves. As I waded into the water I reached down and swirled my fingertips in the water and it unexpectedly giggled at me!

I was surprised, delighted and completely caught up in the beauty and uniqueness of the river. As I waded into the river it started flowing through me.

It flowed through my heart and mind. I could feel the river literally washing away the darkened memories in my life.

As I watched, I could see all the ill experiences from my past drifting down the river. As they drifted into the distance the river became extremely turbulent, violently pulling all the unwanted experiences in my life, down to the bottom of the river. Since that day, the emotions of those unhappy experiences seem like a faint meaningless haze of the past. Now, whenever they try to raise their ugly head, I just praise God and watch them disappear beneath the rivers of praise in my heart."

> *"...Behold, I extend peace to her like a river,*
> *And the glory of the nations like*
> *an overflowing stream..."*
> *(Isaiah 66:12)*

What an awesome God we serve! Tamera and I have had to work through some very troubling experiences in both our lives. Yet today, we stand in the realization that tormenting memories from the past are now just a micro image of what used to be.

This passage in Revelations reads like this,

> *"Then he showed me a river of the water of life, clear as crystal, coming from the throne of God and of the Lamb, in the middle of its street. On either side of the river was the tree of life, bearing twelve kinds of fruit, yielding its fruit every month; and the leaves of the tree were for the healing of the nations."*
> *(Revelations 22:1-2)*

Supernatural Reset #10

I invite you to enter into this river of life. Though you might not be able to see this river with your natural eyes, it is nonetheless inside of you, in your heart. So before moving onto the next chapter of this book, I invite you to read through these few passages of scripture again in **Revelations 22**.

Like Tamera, your imagination is key to exercising your heart in the kingdom of God. Again, this is not to say you are not already free or cleansed by the blood of the Lamb. As you might already know, simple exercises of faith like this can often create a landmark in your heart and mind, thus leave an everlasting revelation of the cleansing power of God in your life.

Let me assure you, there is no end to what God will do in your life through this simple act of faith.

In the eyes of your Father, you are wonderful, powerful and glorious!

_____

_____

_____

_____

_____

_____

_____

_____

_____

_____

_____

_____

_____

_____

_____

_____

_____

_____

The Altar of Heaven

During a previous encounter I had in heaven, there was an altar positioned in the center of the throne room of God.

As I approached the altar, I heard the Lord say, **"Come and lie down on this altar."** When I did, I began to sing this song, "Slay me with your love...slay me with your grace... slay me with your glory and desire..."

I was reminded of the words of Paul when he wrote,

> *"Therefore, I urge you, brethren, by the mercies of God, to present your bodies a living and holy sacrifice, acceptable to God, which is your spiritual service of worship. And do not be conformed to this world, but be transformed by the renewing of your mind, so that you may prove what the will of God is, that which is good and acceptable and perfect."*
> *(Romans 12:1-2)*

During this encounter, I had a sense that my entire being was being transported into another time, into another age, into another mind. It was as though every obstruction from my past was being wiped away. It felt as though the hands of God were surgically removing my old heart and replacing it with a new one. Afterwards, I had a much greater sense of God's love and his purpose and intent for my life.

During this encounter, I could read the mysteries of God on the tablet of my own heart. Since then I have come to realize we don't just have a scroll of identity in heaven, but we are a living scroll of heaven on Earth.

In the book of **Hebrews**, we read,

"This is the covenant that I will make with them,
after those days, says the Lord:
I will put My laws upon their heart,
And on their mind I will write them,"
He then says, and their sins and their lawless deeds,
I will remember no more."
(Hebrews 10:16)

If God could put his laws upon our heart and mind under an old covenant, how much more can he put his words and plans in our hearts and mind under a new covenant through Jesus Christ? Therefore, the purpose and destiny of God for our life is already in us, we just need to discover what that is. In addition,

The love of God in me became so intense that it overrode any false barriers or illusions of separation. I knew I was in him and he was in me. For the first time I felt like I really knew what Paul was speaking of when he wrote,

"Let this mind be in you which was also in Christ
Jesus, who, being in the form of God, did not consider
it robbery to be equal with God..."
(Romans 2:5-6)

Prior to this experience, I constantly labored trying to know the will of God for my life. Now it's as if I have always known. Sometimes it's hard for me to make the distinction between not having known the will of God for me versus having known it all the time. In other words, it's as though I have always known God's divine intent for my life. In addition, many disturbing moments in my past seemingly just disappeared. As goofy as it might sound, it was like going through a supernatural carwash, except that it cleans you from the inside out. Though my aim is not to turn the renewing of your mind into a one-time event, I do want to make one thing very clear, there is an actual alter in the throne room of God awaiting your arrival.

The good news is you can frequent this heavenly place of service and worship as often as you like. There is an extended invitation from Father toward anyone who truly wants to be set free from an old mindset and be delivered into an increasing revelation of the heart and mind of God. In this place, depreciating memories and experiences from former years are eradicated. As a result, the eternal nature of Jesus Christ is enthroned in your heart.

Supernatural Reset #11

Here is another prophetic declaration:

The altar of heaven is in you, in your heart. The love of God is enthroned in you and you in him. The seat of glory is the residence of his love and desire toward you. You are literally the enthronement of heaven on Earth.

The revelation of *"old things passing away and all things becoming new"* is the process of growing up into the revelation of his love, which overrides every deceptive work of darkness.

_____

_____

_____

Chapter 7

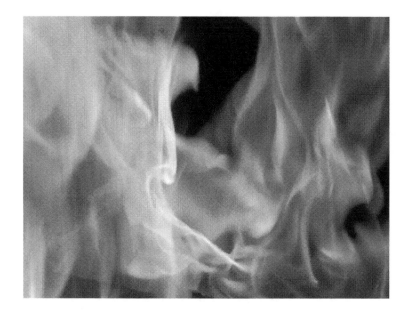

The Fire of God

I want to speak to you about the fire of God and how this supernatural fire has played an important role in consuming the works of the enemy in my life. Afterwards, I will share another major scientific breakthrough that is beyond the comprehension of most. Whether it's a physical issue in the body or burning away unwanted memories, there is no end to what the fire of God can do. Throughout the bible, the fire of God is, and has always been, a major instrument for dealing with the works of the enemy. It's also served as an intense portal to empowering the people of God.

I could write an entire book on all the fiery examples in the bible. In order to transition you into the revelation of this next thought, I feel it is necessary to have you meditate on the following scriptures to acclimate you to this heavenly fire.

After the fall of man, a cherubim and fiery sword was used to guard the entrance to Eden.
Genesis 3:24

The Lord rained fire and brimstone on Sodom and Gomorrah.
Genesis 19:24

God consumed Elijah's offering with fire.
1Kings 18:38

"Smoke went up out of His nostrils fire from His mouth..."
2Samuel 22:9

"Moses stretched out his staff toward the sky, and the LORD sent thunder and hail, and fire ran down to the earth..."
Exodus 9:23

Reveals the Son of God as having eyes like a flame of fire.
Revelation 2:18

Gives us peek into the throne of God where there are flashes of lightning, thunder and seven lamps of fire, which are the seven spirits of God.
Revelation 4:5

*Speaks about tongues as of fire appearing and resting on
each one of the disciples in the upper room.
Acts 2:3-4*

As you can see, the fiery possibilities of God's are endless.

I want to make another prophetic declaration.

*In 2018, and in the years to come, you can expect to see
the fire of God demonstrated in unimaginable ways. As
our hearts and minds continue on the path of spiritual
restoration, especially in the area of sonship, the world
around us will supernaturally advance into the image and
likeness of God at untold levels. I believe 2018 will be
marked as another historical year of extreme change, not
for the worse, but for the better.*

*While it is common for changes to reveal themselves each
year, there are years and seasons in history when an
intense acceleration becomes historically apparent. In
addition, I have been speaking about the year, 2020, and
how it will manifest a level of spiritual maturity that will
surpass anything we have ever witnessed before. In a
large sense, I firmly believe being set free from unwanted
experiences from the past will be key to millions of people
unlocking the future destiny of God for their lives.*

The Fire of Heaven

For decades, countless people have spiritually experienced
the fire of God. Many have testified to the fire of God
healing their bodies. Others who minister in the gift of
healing have said their hands felt like they were on fire.
On occasion, I have experienced these same effects while

prophetically ministering to others. All the above describe how the fire of God has revealed itself through the ages. Without veering too far off forgetting the past, I would like to share a supernatural encounter I had with the fire of God.

Several years ago, I tripped on the concrete edge of my front porch. Using my hands to break my fall, I fractured my left wrist in two different places. My daughter Amber, who is an ER nurse, was present when I went to the emergency room at the hospital.

They took some x-rays and then waited for an orthopedic surgeon to view them. After viewing the images, it was confirmed that I had multiple fractures in my left wrist. They put my arm in a temporary cast and made an appointment for me to see an orthopedic doctor. Fortunately, they were able to get me in within a few days.

On the morning of my appointment, I went downstairs to read and spend some personal time with the Lord. Shortly into my time, I put the book aside and began to pray. Suddenly in my mind's eye, I could see what looked like one of those old-time clay ovens. It appeared to be about four feet off the floor with a fire burning inside. I was a bit surprised and wasn't sure if what I was seeing was real. As odd as it sounds, I felt prompted to put my hand in the fire. With little hesitation, I stretched out my left arm and put it into the burning blaze. To my surprise, the fire was not hot. So, I repeatedly put my arm in and out of the fire. I remember thinking, "The fire is not hot. Why isn't the fire hot?"

Suddenly, I found myself standing on a pathway laid with white stones, with a long wall of fire burning on each side of me. Again, seemingly without any hesitation, I stretched out my arms like an eagle spreading its wings. Amazingly, this fire was not hot either. Its color was mixed with mostly blue and green and maybe just a tint of yellow and red, but for the most part it was a blue-green blaze of fire that burned at least a couple of feet taller than me, which meant it was every bit of eight feet high.

As I walked down the pathway moving my arms through the fire, to my surprise it felt more like water mixed with light. Though it looked like a burning wall of hot fire, to the touch, it was very cool and soothing. It was obviously unlike any fire I had ever experienced before.

In the intensity of the moment, I was suddenly hit with the awareness of time. Just as quickly as this crazy encounter began, it ended. "What time is it? I thought." Looking at the clock on the mantle in front of me, I realized my doctor appointment was only thirty minutes away.

It's A Miracle

When I arrived at my appointment they took me to a back room, removed the temporary support from my hand and took new x-rays. Shortly thereafter a nurse came and took me to where the doctor was viewing my x-rays pinned to a screen above his head.

Looking up he said, "The x-ray on the left is the one they took at the hospital and the one on the right is the one we took here. As you can see, there are two hairline fractures here on the left x-ray, but on the right x-ray, which is the one we just took, there is just a faint shadow of where the fractures should be."

"Wow," I replied. "That seems a bit unusual."

"Yes," the doctor replied, "It is."

"So, why do you think they are so different?" I asked.

"Hmmm...it's hard to say. It could be the one from the hospital is just a poor exposure."

"But couldn't you say that about the one you just took as well?" I asked.

"Possibly." he replied.

"I also see, you have a few bone spurs on this wrist from a previous injury. Those must be very painful."

"Now that you say that, I do remember having issues with stiffness in my wrist every time I would play my guitar or other similar activities. But I just realized I have not felt that for a quite a while now."

"Isn't that unusual too?" I asked.

Looking a bit puzzled, at my response, he quickly adjusted his composure and said, "Well, regardless, for whatever reason, it appears what might have been before isn't that way now. And as you say, the spurs are not causing you any pain. Though that is a bit puzzling as well, it is a good thing for you."

Shutting off the light, the doctor pulled the x-rays down from the screen and said, "The only thing I know to do is release you into your own care and if something changes down the road you can make another appointment."

After leaving the clinic, I got into my car and sat there, wondering what just happened. I was struck with an undeniable reality. The fiery experience I had a few hours earlier wasn't my imagination, it was the real deal. Like Shadrach, Meshach and Abednego in the Bible, who encountered the supernatural presence of God in the fire, I had just encountered the miraculous healing fire of God.

I remember thinking, fire in heaven and fire on Earth burn at a different frequency. Natural fire is a destructive force that requires oxygen, fuel and heat. However, the fire of the spirit is not comprised of the laws of physics. Moses experienced this same fire in a very unique way.

> *"The angel of the Lord appeared to him in a blazing fire from the midst of a bush; and he looked, and the bush was burning with fire, yet the bush was not consumed."*
> *(Exodus 3:2)*

Are you seeing this? The fire Moses experienced didn't just have God in it, but it was God. Just like the *"Word became flesh and dwelt among us"* so this burning flame of glory became the likeness of God, manifesting his intent and desire toward Moses. In this same likeness, by the Spirit of God, in conjunction to being the light of the world, we are also the fire of God.

> *"And of the angels He says,*
> *'Who makes His angels winds*
> *and His ministers a flame of fire?"*
> *(Hebrews 1:7)*

Therefore, in much the same way, this same supernatural fire can heal the physical body can also heal unwanted memories.

The River of Fire

I would like to share one more experience that specifically relates to the "river of fire." In **Revelation 4**, John saw the Lord sitting on a throne in heaven and around the throne are twenty-four elders, four living creatures and many other profound glorious expressions of the glory of Jesus Christ. John describes this glorious enthronement as a fixed or stationary throne in the kingdom of God. In **Revelation 22**, John also writes about the river of life flowing from the throne of God. This is the same river Tamera wrote about in a previous chapter of this book. Daniel had a throne room experience as well. However, Daniel saw thrones supernaturally being set up right before his eyes.

> *"I kept looking*
> *Until thrones were set up,*
> *And the Ancient of Days took His seat.*
> *His vesture was like white snow*
> *and the hair of His head like pure wool.*
> *His throne was flames of fire,*
> *Its wheels were a burning fire."*

> *"A river of fire was flowing*
> *And coming out from before Him;*
> *Thousands upon thousands were attending Him,*
> *And myriads upon myriads were standing before Him;*
> *the court sat and the books were opened."*
> *(Daniel 7:9-10)*

In this vision, Daniel saw the Ancient of Days (Jesus) taking his seat. He also described the throne as having "wheels of fire" which refers to its mobile authority. Let's look more closely at this astounding throne that Jesus; the Ancient of Days was sitting on. Not only are the wheels made of fire, but also the throne itself is made of "flames of fire". In addition, Daniel saw "a river of fire flowing and coming out from before Him (Jesus)"

So, what does all of this have to do with forgetting the past? There has always been a mystical power in the revelation of the fire of God. This fire of God has everything to do with the burning away of unwanted memories. Remember Tamera's experience with the river of life flowing from the throne of God?

Well, this is much like that, except it is a river of fire. While both rivers evoke life, they do so differently. The river of glory that Tamera experienced, though it had its raging moments, was soothing, peaceful and even playful. My encounter with the river of life was much like Tamera's, minus the giggles. The river of fire is nonetheless a life-giving river as well. However, unlike the previous river, the river of fire is a consuming force of fiery glory that literally devours any work of the enemy.

"Our God is a consuming fire."
(Hebrews 12:29)

Moses knew the fire of the Lord up close and personal.

"The glory of the Lord rested on Mount Sinai, and the cloud covered it for six days; and on the seventh day He called to Moses from the midst of the cloud. And to the eyes of the sons of Israel the

appearance of the glory of the Lord was like a
consuming fire on the mountain top."
(Exodus 24:16-17)

I remember when Tamera and I first engaged with the fire of God together. I had her read with me the fiery passages I just noted in Daniel, chapter 7. Afterwards, by faith, through our sanctified imagination, we both stepped into this raging fire flowing from the throne of the Ancient of Days. Remember, Tamera described her encounter with the river of life as "passing right through her. At the same time, it washed through her mind cleansing it from previous unwanted experiences."

This time, together, as we entered into the river of fire, it was as though the inward parts of our being were set ablaze. Like my previous encounter with the fire of God the flames were not hot to the touch, but very comforting and healing. We were both impacted by an intense red-hot desire for God's love. It felt as though a liquid of burning love was flowing through the deepest parts of our being. It certainly gave us both a whole new understanding of the "consuming fire of God." After discussing our initial encounter with the river of fire, we both realized was that we ourselves became one with the fire of God. We literally became "flames of fire."

"He makes the winds His messengers,
Flaming fire His ministers."
Psalms 104:4

Since then, I've had numerous encounters with the fire of God, which have resulted in unwanted memories being set aflame and consumed, as though they were never a part of my life.

Supernatural Reset #12

Before you leave this chapter, I want to encourage you to go back and read the seventh chapter of Daniel again. This time, ask the Lord to lead you into the burning river of his love. I am confident; you will never be the same again.

For those of you who would like a little help engaging with the river of fire, I have a fire CD that was created out of a spontaneous moment in worship. It's titled, "Rivers of Fire" which is available on our website. **(mticenter.com)**

_____

_____

_____

_____

_____

_____

_____

_____

_____

_____

_____

_____

_____

_____

_____

_____

Chapter 8

Light, Sound, and Worship

You Are the Light

In the early mid 2000's we would often come together for a time of worship. We generally would meet around 6:00AM, prior to everyone heading off to work. There were times when it would feel as though my entire being was going through some kind of biological transformation. Each encounter was marked with a surge of electrifying energy that would rise up on the inside of me. Over a period of time, I continued to experience a significant renewing in my heart, mind and body. Nikola Tesla long believed that the entire atmosphere around us was filled with some sort of super charged field of energy.

He writes,

"If you want to find the secrets of the universe, think in terms of energy, frequency and vibration." Nikola Tesla

Again, he writes,

"The day science begins to study non-physical phenomena, it will make more progress in one decade than in all the previous centuries of its existence." Nikola Tesla

Paul describes it like this,

"For by (through) Him all things were created, both in the heavens and on earth, visible and invisible, whether thrones or dominions or rulers or authorities—all things have been created through Him and for Him. He is before all things, and in Him all things hold together."
(Colossians 1:16-17)

Though my personal experiences were a by-product of the light of God in me, many now realize the world of solid matter is not really solid after all. If you magnified your cells down to their atoms you would quickly realize you are made of subtle energy fields of light. The world of physics is continually discovering that the basic building blocks of energy are indeed light and sound.

When Jesus said, *"You are the light of the world"* he wasn't just speaking about some spiritual metaphor. We are literally made up of the light of God, which is the love of God. We are the light of the world. Before too long, I increasingly became aware that previous regretted experiences in my heart and mind had soon become faint distant memories. The unwanted residue from my past had been reduced to a small silhouette of what used to be me.

Switching Off the Past

For years, I have prophetically spoken about major breakthroughs concerning light. Whether on Earth or in the heavens above, the light of God has and will always be the beginning and the end.

The final frontier will not be chaos, but an eventual eternal divine order that will place all of creation right smack in the middle of the light of God's glory.

This means everything in the natural realm is destined to come under the auspices of God's eternal light. The apostle John saw this coming glory in his day.

> *Then the seventh angel sounded; and there were loud voices in heaven, saying, "The kingdom of the world has become the kingdom of our Lord and of His Christ; and He will reign forever and ever."*
> *(Revelations 11:15)*

When you are seated in heavenly places, you can easily see that the final and great awakening is literally the finger of God switching on the eternal light of his love, thus revealing his eternal nature in his sons and daughters. Medical science is quickly coming into some amazing new discoveries in the area of memories. Much of the science world has discovered that memories can be turned off as easily as flipping a light switch to the off position. Since 2010, scientists have made some major breakthroughs in controlling the brain with light technology.

Richard Gray, is a science correspondent for **"The Telegraph"** which is a national British daily broadsheet newspaper published in London by **Telegraph Media Group** and distributed across the United Kingdom and internationally.

On June 17, 2012 Richard Gray writes,

"Scientists have developed a way of using pulses of light to turn the brain cells that control our everyday actions and thoughts on or off at will. It provides a way of controlling the brain in a way that was never possible before."

He goes on to say,

"This technology promises to provide revolutionary new treatments for diseases that are notoriously difficult to control such as Epilepsy, Alzheimer's disease and psychiatric illnesses. It could even help people make new memories."

Of course, it's important to know whenever science leans into "cell manipulation" it can create quite a controversy in the medical world because not every course of action in this arena is necessarily a good one. Nonetheless, the potential of possibilities in the area of turning off traumatic memories, for many, are a welcoming reality.

In August of 2017, a recent headline in **Scientific American** reads,

"Scientists Use Light to Turn Off Autism in lab testing"

It goes on to say,

"Turning on a set of neurons that dampen brain activity improves social behavior in mice that model autistic behavior; turning off neurons that excite brain activity does the same thing. The work relies on a technique called optogenetics that Karl Deisseroth, professor of bioengineering and psychiatry at Stanford University in California and his team pioneered. In this technique, researchers engineer mice to express light-sensitive proteins called opsins. They then shine light into the mice's brains to turn certain neurons on or off."

Every time I hear about advances such as this my spiritual radar always detects something beyond the natural realm. If natural frequencies of light have the ability to switch off or transpose unhealthy cells into good ones, how much more can the light of God align our physical bodies to his eternal intent? Because of the light of God's love working in us, the cells of our bodies are continually being swallowed up by immortality.

In heaven, the light of God's love is a supernatural by-product of our eternal state in the kingdom of God.

This same light is part of the fundamental process that transforms our hearts and minds in Christ. Many are discovering pathways or gateways in the kingdom of heaven where unwanted memories or experiences of the past are being recalibrated to the divine nature of Christ.

"Grace and peace be multiplied to you in the knowledge of God and of Jesus our Lord; seeing that His divine power has granted to us everything pertaining to life and godliness, through the true knowledge of Him who called us by His own glory and excellence. For by these He has granted to us His precious and magnificent promises, so that by them you may become partakers of the divine nature, having escaped the corruption that is in the world by lust."
(2Peter 1:2-4)

Forgetting the Past Through Worship

I have had countless experiences engaging with heavenly places. Many of those experiences have come through prophetic worship. For me, prophetic worship is the construct of songs that come from a spontaneous response to the spirit of God.

I have practiced this method of worship for over 25 years. Through song I have journeyed into the heavenly realms. Each journey has afforded me the ability to see Earth from the perspective of heaven.

Before I dive into the spiritual side of how to override unwanted memories through the sound of worship, lets take a brief look at the science of how memory and sound are connected. It's certainly no surprise that a song or a certain sound can trigger vivid memories. Those moments can transport you back through time and space. Sounds, specifically music, have the ability to raise old emotional memories from your past. They can also bring smells and textures to your remembrance. This is because the vibration and frequencies of sound are woven into our neural tapestry, which entwines people with seasons, locations and experiences throughout our lifespan.

What is the neuroscience behind the ability of music to evoke such strong memories? There is a deep neural connection that enables music to reconnect people with past romance, heartbreak, as well as a very wide range of joyful or painful memories. Numerous scientific studies have found that listening to music connects broad neural networks in the brain. This includes areas of the brain that are responsible for actions, emotions and creativity.

Petr Janata, associate professor of psychology at UC Davis "Center for Mind and Brain" writes,

"A piece of familiar music can serve as a soundtrack for creating a mental movie, which plays in a person's head. This same soundtrack can call back memories of past people or places. When it does, an image of those people and places appear in the mind. This study proves there is an association between music and memories."

You may know what it is like to be driving down the highway or sitting in the comfort of your home, listening to a familiar song, then, suddenly having a flashback from the past.

When these memories are unwanted, this might seem like a hopeless emotional merry-go-round of endless unwanted encounters of the "past kind." There is powerful resolution available. In light of all the chapters in this book, as far as I am concerned, I have saved the best for last. It reminds me of the story about the wedding feast Jesus's mother persuaded him to go to.

During this feast, John describes a very important moment.

"Every man serves the good wine first, and when the people have drunk freely, then he serves the poorer wine; but you have kept the good wine until now."
(John 2:10)

Worshiping God through music has, and will always be, one of my greatest pleasures in life. Some of my most intense encounters have come through moments of worshiping God. For me, worship is the place where heaven is increasingly realized on the inside of me. During those times it's as though I am handed a key to unlock the mysteries of God's eternal love, thus overriding the old with the new. Through the frequency and vibration of sound, I have learned to carve out the future in unimaginable ways; cutting away the old and bringing in the new. At the end of the day, I believe the sound of heaven plays an extremely vital role in the reformation of heart and soul, thus the renewing of the mind.

Through the years, I have learned how to take all the unwanted memories of my life and subject them to the glorious resolve of heaven in me. I have watched many of those same memories go through a type of spiritual metamorphosis. It was as though all of the evil intent of the enemy toward me melted like wax in the presence of the Lord. Through the sound of worship, I've seen unwanted images in my mind suddenly being transformed from intense darkness to intense light. As one of the greatest recorded worshipers of all time, David experienced the insurmountable refreshing presence of God's glory over and over again.

Supernatural Reset #13

I invite you to enter into the courts of praise and submit every unwanted memory in your heart and mind to the glorious light of God's love. When you do, I assure you, no, I guarantee, you will never be the same again.

Here are some amazing Psalms written by David, which enabled him to soar above every weight and care in his life.

> *For you, O Lord, have made me glad by what*
> *you have done, I will sing for joy at the*
> *works of your hands.*
> *Psalms 92:4*

> *Bless the Lord, O my soul, and all that is with me,*
> *bless his holy name.*
> *Psalms 103:1*

Let's simplify this even more. We cannot forget the significance of light and sound. We know,

> *"God is light."*
> *(1John 1:5)*

We also know,

> *"His voice is like the sound of many waters."*
> *(Ezekiel 43:2)*

It would be accurate to say that the frequency and vibration of light and sound is love. Therefore, every memory or experience in our life is subject to be overridden by the frequency and vibration of God's love working in us. I am fully convinced that through the sound of worship, our cells vibrate at the frequency of heaven, which is made of the love of God. As a result, we increasingly come under the auspices of the spirit of immortality, which is continually working in us. More great news!

Every unwanted memory in our past can be recalibrated to match the original design and purpose of God for our life.

Let me encourage you to go through all the "spiritual resets" in this book several times until you sense an obvious shift taking place in your heart and mind. I am confident that part of your legacy, your influence in this world, will be to help others transpose and recalibrate any and every unwanted memory in their life. You are amazing!

_____

_____

_____

_____

_____

_____

_____

_____

_____

Check out other books written by
Michael Danforth
www.mticenter.com

next exit

TOTAL RECALL

REMEMBERING THE ORIGINAL YOU

AUTHOR
MICHAEL A. DANFORTH

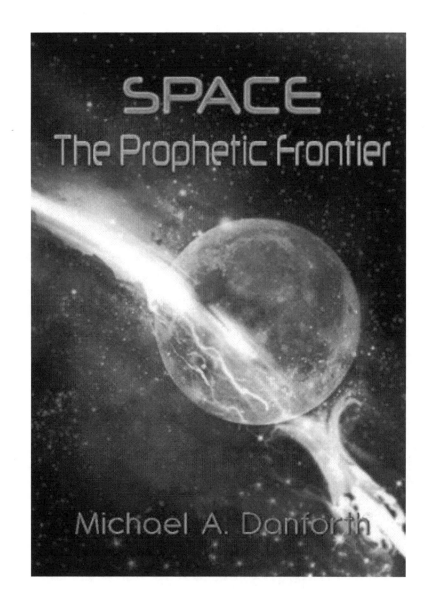

SPACE
The Prophetic Frontier

Michael A. Danforth

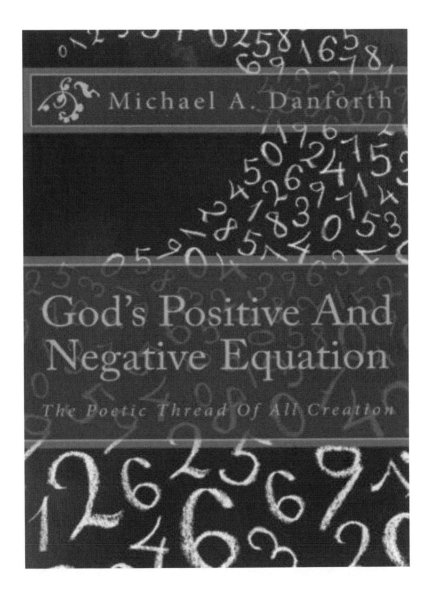

GOD WANTED
A SON

He Was The Word,
Creator Of All Things...

Michael A.
Danforth